AF424042

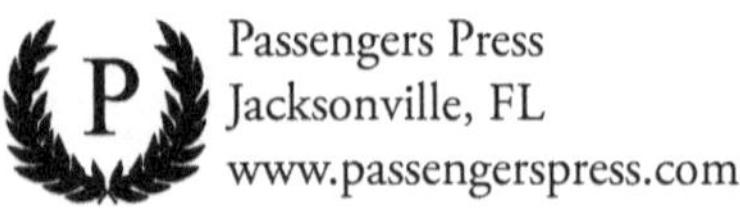

Passengers Press
Jacksonville, FL
www.passengerspress.com

Taleb, Nardine
1st edition.
ISBN: 979-8-218-24953-3

Manuscript Editor: Kimberly Casey
Press Editor-in-Chief: Zac Furlough

Cover photography, design, and book layout: Andreea Ceplinschi

وردة
flower

table of contents

first published in:

a sister — *wildness*
Dear Boy — *SBLAAM*
confessions ghazal — *Tinderbox Poetry Journal*
intentions — *Yes Poetry*
emigration | هجرة — *Emerge Literary Journal*
on street 9 in maadi, cairo — *Mizna*
body of a whale — *Passengers Journal*
the naming of things — *Ghost City Press*
returning home
for quarantine I forget — *Yes Poetry*
with my prayer beads
I pray for bad sushi — *Frontier Poetry*

I want to write different words for you
To invent a language for you alone

Nizar Qabbani

To be made whole
*   by being not a witness,*
but witnessed.

Ada Limon

water

At the dinner party, a horrified
Auntie says: If you allow yourself
everything, you can become
anything.

I count the seconds
before I dismiss
myself. I've started seeking
a kind of home in people but
it's never enough.

Before I meet
God that evening, I rinse
my mouth, nose,
face, arms, hair,
ears, feet.

I want
a home where I am not always
wanting—always alternating
between women, one of
saffron, one of pepper.

Like water I shapeshift,
first a river then a
flooding. To be drowned
by the very thing
that gives you life–
this is not a drill.

I've grown accustomed
to whispering prayers
under my breath
when no one's looking.

Before meeting
a date that evening, I rinse
my mouth of mangoes, pickled
carrots, cinnamon with milk,
apricot juice. I know he'll see
an entire country in my
hair. I close
all the shutters
of my house.

I leave myself on the kitchen floor.

on street 9 in maadi, cairo

We've been warned not to eat the street food,

but we do it anyway, promising ourselves we will

go home after to suffer in our own beds. But the boy

is the color of sandpaper, the kind

girls back in the suburb envy. He strolls with us

to the apartment, tall and bent over, his height

a burden. I pretend not to care, but worshiping

is the kind of thing we do by

default. I take the sides of your eyes like windows

and pull them open. I want to be you. I want to

compare the size of our hips and then write about

our collarbones after. I practice exiting myself

to enter the many bodies of women

I've still yet to become. The skin of fava beans

wedged between my teeth. Residue sand coating

my cheeks. This is the street

where the bread man still heats the bread from the friction

of his hands. Black flies as a side. Cars tailing each other

on each hip of the road like a spine. I'll take the boy

and you can have the west, I joke. You frown,

because like my country, I have the habit

of taking. I recite words I collected

from your mouth to make the boy

smile. And later that night, you call me

every name you know in the book. Every name

except my own.

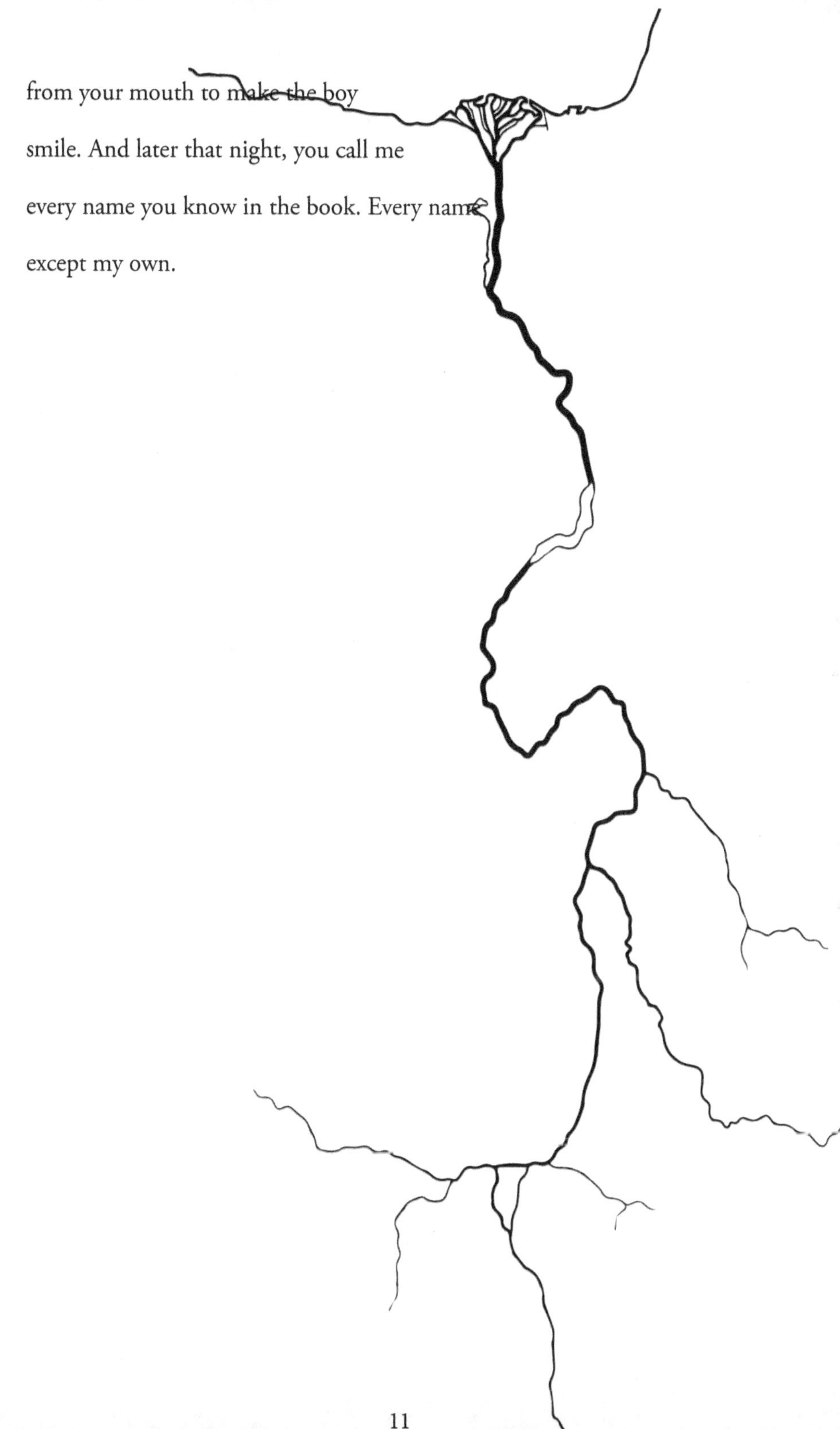

textures of cairo

rumi cheese
wrapped in pita bread
baked on a gas stove
by a woman's hands
that stirred honey
into your mint tea
and the young boys
playing soccer
right under your balcony
kick a ball straight
at you
and asif asif
for the spilled tea
they say
but could you kick
the ball
back?
and the adhan is sounding,
a man with a voice
of many hard lived years
and Abdel Halim Hafez
is singing
a love song
to you
on the TV
the way you imagine
a lover would
and the sun is beating
hot
with warning
and you belong here
in this place that is your shade
but still you can't
stomach
the tap water

I didn't mean to write this poem; I am just trying to land more gently

.

.

.
I don't have much to give. Not the kind
to hand hold, though I have been
lovingly held. At the intersection
of a Cairo street, a boy dies. He is
four. I asked my little cousin who
did it and he said, we all did it. As in:
complicity is its own violence. Remember?
It was a hit and run; they found the small body
in the street. Bruised lip rising from the earth. The parents
couldn't afford a funeral so we gave them the allowance
we usually take to the deli. A dead
boy is just a boy until we make him all of us. After that, we no
longer sneak cubes of sugar in our mouths. We
don't write cute poetry about sunsets. We make porn
from death and some nights are
exactly what nights are: stains. The boy
is just a boy until he is a street name. From afar, he looks
part of the earth and the earth is just a loose tooth. I apologize,
because I stand on the balcony hovering above
like a coward. I'm coming down. I'm only
a boy. Now I am a traffic light.

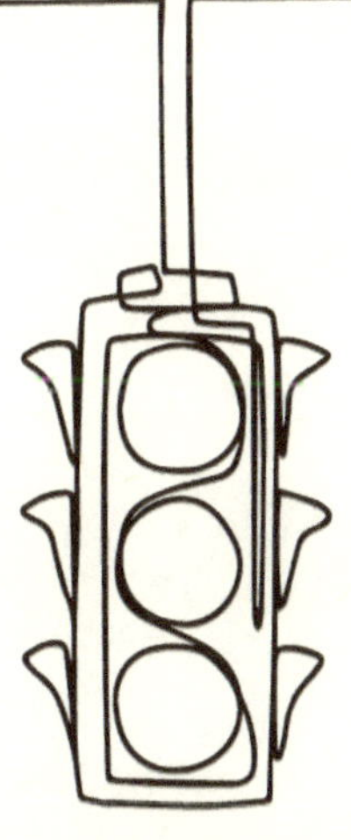

country boy

Does he remember the days I translated Arabic for him, blue flame in daylight?
In his mouth, everything was watered down, as ق turned to ك, ح to ه, yes to
yeah. I danced like a doll to be seen, because I thought it was the only way to
exist, not knowing that I could dictate the song. So I untied bows with my
tongue

        the Arabic

              in my mouth

                  showering

                      meteors.

He asked me, what does سجود mean?
It means prostration   fatigue

    & submission   ~~after him, it really just meant I want to be~~

He made me

                                   ~~forget~~
                         ~~the pulse in Mama's~~
                              ~~laughter~~
                      ~~the dance in Baba's~~
                             ~~accent~~

                  ~~forget the Arabic names for God~~
                      ~~all ninety-nine of them~~

                    ~~Could I add milk to myself~~
                      ~~and become like him~~
                            ~~white clouds~~
                          ~~unquestioned~~
                            ~~and not~~
                            ~~the color~~
                            ~~of sphinx~~
                                 ؟

                              ~~I couldn't~~
                          ~~so instead I~~

mutated, borderless

~~deeply, unconditionally loved.~~

a sister

I couldn't find myself in my aunties, so I opened
up my body, found palms of half-eaten candies, empty
wrappers, melted gum.

A sister says: we must eliminate shame. I bury
myself under arms of snow. Here I am, a fragmented
window, letting other fragmented things pass through me.

Another sister says: my grandmother hands
my mother, my sister, my daughters,
a god concealed in a closed fist.

I seek this god and find him
underneath my tongue. I give people ninety-nine ways
to say my name and they split open.

A sister doesn't know everything. A sister
only knows what is told to her. A sister
is given only quarter-truths, can't even seek herself

in other sisters. When I finally know the questions,
the seeking stops. I skin myself and find,
once concealed, teeth. Like everything veiled,

I want to be known.

body of a whale

I admit that I'm sorry for not acknowledging you at the grocery store, Omar.

You stand at the same cash register, your accent

an incision in the Midwestern chatter. We don't greet each other.

We don't say hello or even *salam*, silence a testimony

that I am closer to you just by way of how we got here.

I see my father in you — in your skin, quick hands, foreignness, knock-

off white Adidas shoes. My mother, is there

in your polite smile, your lowered gaze, your in-

ability to fully twist into the syntax of this country.

Your gaze, avoiding, I

set *The New Yorker* on your counter, the hair products

to dampen the curls. This is how I twisted: I couldn't find

the fava beans my mother wanted to make an Egyptian breakfast, or perhaps

I chose not to look for fear I would also have to get the cumin.

You say, straight face, *Want bag?*

Omar, I am a white man in the body of an Arab girl.

I am a white girl in the body of an Arab girl.

I am an Arab girl in the body of a white man in the body

of a white girl in the body of america, america with the body

of a whale, america with the body of a refugee, america with the body of

an Arab girl, stepping into a room full of wide eyes and blackholes. It is hard

to see the world without america in my body. I want a day

where I'm not written off by curious eyes.

Now you give me a receipt and so simply you're tugging on history.

I promise I'll tell you right, yes, I'll take a bag,

I'll take this whale headed nowhere, nowhere

still being somewhere to belong to, still ahead of us, some kind of ocean.

confessions ghazal

At eighteen, the aunties follow me with their eyes, each a curious tongue

I squirm through a hello, behind a smile and a sweet tongue.

I shove booty shorts in the back of a drawer, everybody's a snake, with a divulging

I stumble through errors, I bake in daylight, beg its god to accept my tongue.

I was born into a contradicting culture that presses

itself against me and asks me to remember its tongue

and it takes me years and years to not flinch at the prayer call

My friends hear it and don't run. How many nights have I wished for another

Wished for shameless imperfection and fearless embrace of desire? In secret

I kiss the holy book and it blushes, and God asks for me one evening, a confession tongue

tongue?

on His tongue.

intentions

I will never get married, I say to Mama.
She replies, InshAllah
the word trailing after her every sentence
through pursed lips.

She pulls the vowels of InshAllah by their ears
and her tone shifts, as she summons God.
Nothing, she says, is only of our will,
the dead mouse in our basement, for instance,
a credit to the Evil Eye
or true love, a credit to the Right Time.

Even our morning rise cannot be a fluke,
God dropping souls back into bodies
like coins into empty glass jars.

Down on our knees, our bodies
are the vessels for the prayers
we won't admit out loud
and maybe, what all mothers
want to do is birth more
mothers and so

on the MRI scan when my pelvic
lights up, an unwomanly thing,
the size of a baseball
I want to know
if I don't become a mother
InshAllah can I still become an arm?

If I don't become a home,
InshAllah is it okay to be
half woman, half water?

emigration | هجرة

I move differently now, with my hands
nestled into the valley of my hips
my lips blush bubblegum pink my eyes two   watchful moons
I smile with her smile and open

        the door of new land

            with her hands

                            Over the years   I've watched countries
                    emerge from her body's once flat land. I'd like to roll
                    her back into my own
                    into the safety   of my body   her birth place
                                    where strangers
                    do not mispronounce her name   and the word
                    "love" is not watered down   I wish to tell her
                    stay here & be content   out there
                    your hair will be touched by someone else

at twenty-five I unlearned my first language
with his body   white   color of the inside of
a peach   I tried to locate myself
outside of myself

        I was so naive I forgot

            to tell him the translation of my name

                    I have a girl   woman once the size of my palm
                    I am a temple now   sometimes
                            cracked   at the sides
                    still standing   people come to admire
                    the preservation of my skin   colors of sand &
                    heritage   in her absence   I tell them come
                    come & take   I am looking to give love as I have
                    always done   drink water   from my bare hands
                    and   sleep   tucked under my pits   I know you
                    are just looking for belonging   my youth has been
                    resurrected elsewhere   if you visit her   you will see
                    there is a God

morning prayer

I don't want to know
the sound of a toilet flush
jarring me awake at 2 am
if it isn't you
shuffling out of the bathroom
chanting God's name
to the angels: ya rab al-
alameen ya kareem.

I don't want to know old age
if it isn't your skin
golden and wrinkled,
if it isn't your
hair, a collapsing mop
once youthful,
if it isn't your knees
weak but still able.

I don't want to know
the feel of our living
room without you
in it, your legs
splayed out in front of you,
taking up space,
anchored towards
Mecca.

I don't want to know a prayer
if it isn't you who taught it to me,
advice, if it isn't you who
gave it to me,
a song, if it isn't belted out
by your restless throat.

I don't want to know
how else to arrive at a place
without camouflaging the pain
of your absence,
now that I know how
to walk into a room
and blend into it.

And now that I know
how to conceal,
I am no longer a young girl,
and every conversation in prayer
has your name in it.

evening prayer

When I remember my grandmother,
now just a name cupped
in my hands, I know
she wouldn't be impressed
with me. But she never told
me, in my defense, if it's true
that I am at my best
when I am starving, sleep
deprived and unfastened
to time. I love too
easily, and a boy finds me, un-
curls me like a strand of hair
around his forefinger
held up as if in
shahada. Yes, he knows
all the holy verses. In fact,
he can recite the holy book
in the open air, recite ar-
rahman ar-raheem.
He silently watches
women passing by
at the cafe, with my leg
propped up on his. He insists
I try the sparkling water; he insists
I will love it. It is true,
I will love it. But the Arabic
does not make him a sheikh,
does not mean his hands
are safe.

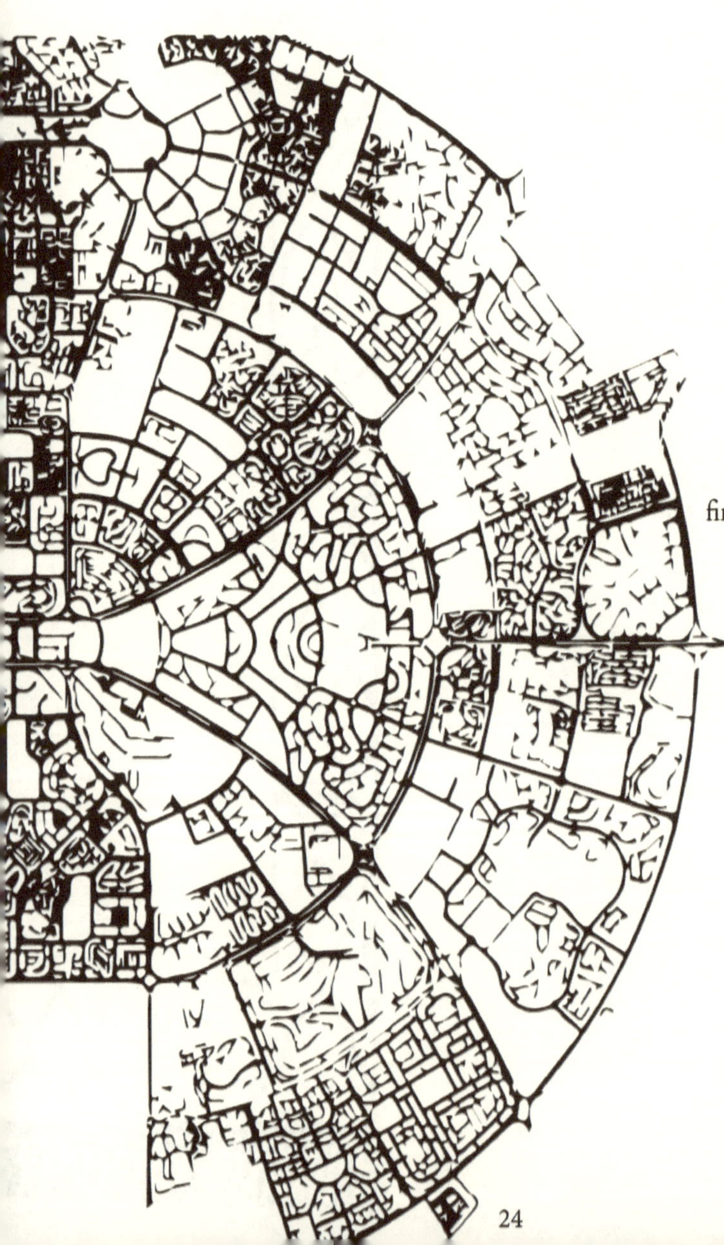

water II (rinse, repeat)

Before meeting
God that evening, I rinse
the mouth, nose,
face, arms, hair,
ears, then feet.

I won't forget
but I forgive
myself for the years
I omitted my love
for stuffed pigeon
and grape leaves.

In conversation
about food,
I talk instead about
what I can't
have,
about how
closer to thirty
the same streets
I've driven
since sixteen
finally look like home.

These streetlights,
no longer
blinking
as three
disapproving eyes.

This winding road,
throat of turmeric,

yes,
I can become
anything.

the naming of things

I.   This is how I imagine you:
sitting on a hill, picturing God as a tree,
reaching for me like a fountain of water
craving for palms

I named you, as all real
things should be named: lover,
partner, hope, home, unlocked
door, dark basement, a fleeting
thought, a moment's
dinner, a word, a trashed lyric
a wound   I open & open

II.   You didn't know how to pray.
You *thought* you did.

Consider this: looking as a form of prayer. Everywhere we turn
with our eyes, we are trying to escape where we are. I looked at
you long and hard once, you looked
back.

Language ruins everything, you said. Don't name. Just observe.

III.   The women in my family are pillars.
We are taught to hold. On a cold day,
I held you up, while you grieved. I carried grief,
dead skin, like an embrace. I knew we were

Nothing.

I hope you didn't notice, after you'd driven off,
that I had left my hands in your backseat.

IV.

I'll write you out of me, sprinting away from — or towards
truth. I only know language and how it peels, its commas
the edges of a knife. I try on all the mouths of my women
to hear your name again and again in different tones. My body
stops being a thing of worship, instead becomes
an ocean with doors

birthmark

I was stranded, once, in the belly of a

whale. I found a birthmark

on the back of my leg, discovering

I'm not just another set

of hands. This is no secret.

I had to move further away

from myself to want myself

back. Thinking: not only

submission but submersion

not only worship but water.

For years upon years

I was terrified,

not of the storm,

but of what I would do

when it came. After –

I taught myself

when to bend.

I fixed the ravaged

birdhouse in my backyard

with my own two hands. By next day,

more birds arrived.

even poetry can't open a window for me today

on my way to work / I found myself in the arms of a poem / and turned the car
to go back home / I think about joy often / I'm reckless with it / like that car on
fire, stopped along I-480 / its flames a caution, a pair of outstretched hands / I
remembered how there are places in my body that fail me like that / my chest
/ knees / back of the neck / holding memories when memories are costly / the
truth is that everyday there is a stain of you / sitting in the back of my car in
front of Lake Erie / the trunk wide open / on a cold Cleveland day / and there
are seagulls making waves above us / ignorant to weather warnings / aren't we, ya
dunya / like little boys and girls comfortable in our illusions / confusing longing
for love / that body with no grave / I read in the holy book / the world is made
up / of dreams and play / so I imagine myself a poem / I imagine myself the
flame inside the hood / I imagine myself / one day / existing / a car no longer in
reverse

baklava

On a Ramadan night, she does not touch
the baklava, too sweet and too addictive,
the last thing she ate with her last
true love. When she is talking
with an auntie at a party, she wants
to break out into poem. She decides to recite:
I run to you and I find that you had always been
there: I just had to turn around. There
you are, unearthed: like a cheek waiting
to be kissed. And the auntie
is in tears, remembering
her own past, and the poem becomes a memory,
which is, of course, a home.

           The girl is seeking
something – to be seen, perhaps,
the way that Medjool dates want to be
seen, sitting on the counter, a minute
before breaking fast, the ending
of hunger. Fasting doesn't bother her –
she's been hungry for much longer than that.
Whatever you're seeking, says the auntie,
will come when you stop
seeking it.

But what if seeking
is the truest human act? What if seeking
is something you do to convince yourself
you are alive?

with my prayer beads I pray for bad sushi

"The angel caught me (forcefully) and pressed me so hard that I could not bear it any more. He then released me and again asked me to read and I replied, 'I do not know how to read.'"

-Muhammad ibn Isma'il al-Bukhari

Sometimes, I speak
only out of need to hear
longing. The prayer beads just
fingers to hold. Little ears
to God. A child
has a tantrum at my feet and I feed
him mouthfuls of language
to explain himself. How I try to quench
my own longing by pressing
words against other people's gums. How
the same space I seek poetry
is where I also seek God. I am not
even sure what I'm praying for, but there is
a little bit of myself
in the unanswered things, like: I wish
to be reunited with my dead. I wish
for bad sushi. I wish
for lust that drains. I wish
for cold coffee, and plants
that only last a week, and rain
we can't drink. I'm on my way
to submissiveness but first
I must get through
myself. There are many things
I've loved that I've learned
to lose. So I wedge
the prayer beads
inside my throat. READ,
said God,
I read.

returning home I forget

how frequently the prayer call fumbles
out of the computer and never really seems
to end, especially when I'm on work calls
or Facetime with friends or in prostration
to a slice of dark chocolate cake. I'm coming,
God, but on my way to you I loved the world
a little less, couldn't find all the reasons I danced
in drugstore aisles or sang unrestrained in the car
with my windows down. I listen with intention
to the small things: Mama brewing
coffee; Baba chatting about almonds
being in the plum family. Living in the unknown
is a talent. And I do it unwillingly.
My pink childhood walls are chipping,
the chippings questioning my womanhood:
Q: Where are you headed?
A: Wherever Mama's footsteps
are imprinting. Wherever
Babas are humming. Wherever
coffee is brewing. Wherever
walls are chipping. Wherever
pantries are filling. Wherever
eyes are closed and palms
are open.

acknowledgements

I came from a family of language and stories and my family continues to grow.

I am so grateful for the Passengers Press family, for Zac Furlough, whose journal published one of my very first pieces, and for my incredible editor Kimberly Casey who answered my endless questions and guided me in the vision of this chapbook. Thank you to Andreea Ceplinschi, whose cover art for this book has exceeded any expectations I've ever had.

Many thanks to the various journals who accepted my poems and gave me the momentum to continue writing. Thank you to the many talented friends who explored the manuscript with me for any errors or hidden meanings: J.C., Noura, Monica, and Karen. I continue to be in awe of poetry because of your work, of how we can move art so that it moves us. And to also listen to what's already there.

To Sonia Feldman: I'm grateful to be on this writing journey with you. No mercy, keep writing! To Ghinwa Jawhari: I've always looked up to you and am so thankful for your support of my creative work.

I must thank my friends who I can talk about for hours and have always been there to uplift me. Thank you for reciting my lines to me, even when I forget that it was I who wrote them.

To my mother, Nermin, for reading to me as a kid and introducing me to my second love (writing) – you are, of course, my first love. My dad, Mohamed, your curiosity about the world makes me smile. To approach the world with a childlike wonder, even when it gets hard–you taught me to embody that. My brother, Kareem, I've driven you crazy enough and you're still patient with me. I'm sorry for never closing the toothpaste cap properly.

Thank you to writers and friends across many workshops, journals, and poetry readings I've met–for teaching me that the world is always seeking to be understood. You are my flowers.